HI5IVE

The Simplest
Computer Language

A SiComplex Book

HI5IVE

Table of Contents

HI5IVE

HI5IVE

The Approach
To Creating the Simplest Computer Language

Every computer has to have a Language in which to write the applications and operating system. [Most computers use several Languages.] It would be nice if that Language were simple enough to use that if you needed to do something simple that wasn't provided for by the computer, you could whip up a little application to do that for you in a matter of minutes. And, even if you needed to do something complex, you could still use this same simple-to-use Language.

A computer Programming Language is a group of Commands which tell the computer what to do.

If you could devise the simplest computer Language possible, how would you go about it? Perhaps you'd say, "Who needs a computer Language?" Well computer Languages are used to write all those apps you use. Computer Languages are used to write websites. And having a computer Language available to do simple tasks that aren't available by clicking somewhere in an app, would come in handy.

Perhaps you'd come up with a graphical or picture based Language. But sometimes it would be nice to just type a few simple Statements and have your computer do what you want. Perhaps your computer Language would combine Statements, images, and cursor or finger motions into one simple Language.

Dale Stubbart   YellowBearJourneys.com

HI5IVE

My approach to creating the simplest computer Programming Language was to look at all the Commands or Statements in various Programming Languages and combine those that did basically the same thing, thus reducing the number of Commands and simplifying the Language. Then I came up with a syntax for the resulting Commands that was simple and consistent across the Commands. (Majoring in both Language and Computer Science in college came in handy.)

Licensing

HI5IVE

The Purpose
Why Develop another Computer Language

When I was in graduate school in 1981, my advisor wanted me to write my master's thesis developing a PC version of the Ada Programming Language. The head of the department threw out my thesis because I had not put forth a valid reason for developing "yet another computer Language". There have been many computer Languages created since then. Some of the older computer Languages have become obsolete, but some like COBOL are still widely used. Ada is now used mainly for Military and other "mission critical" systems like Aviation.

The US military was responsible for overseeing the development of COBOL, which first became a computer Language in 1960. Twenty years later, the military developed Ada to replace COBOL. COBOL was widely adopted by businesses. Ada never became that popular.

The most popular Languages these days (2015) are Java, Python, C (and variations of C), Ruby, Javascript, PHP, SQL, HTML, and CSS. I'm not seeing COBOL or Ada in this list.

So, why introduce another computer Language to the list of at least 600 computer Languages already in existence, even if not all of those 600 are still in use?

Few, if any of those 600 Languages are what I would call simple. And very few, if any have simple, consistent syntax rules that apply across all the Commands. And, having a computer Language available to create task shortcuts, comes in handy.

HI5IVE

Background and Evolution

In 1972, in undergraduate studies, one of my professors taught us the basics of all computer Languages by showing us a computer Language he had designed on paper. This computer Language had four Commands – MOVE, IF, COMPUTE, and PRINT. Those Commands may have had other names, I don't remember, but that's basically what they did. The Language was not viable as a functioning Programming Language at that time because there was no way to proceed from one Command to the next. Subsequent classes had the task of making that Language a functioning Programming Language. I never heard what happened with that Programming Language. I'm fairly certain it never made it beyond the campus of that college.

His Programming Language started out with only four Commands. Others were added in the effort to make it a functioning Language.

In the early 1990's, drawing on what I learned from that course, I designed a new computer Language with the fewest possible number of Commands or Statements. All the Statements had the same format which helped keep the syntax simple and allowed you to be prompted for the next part of the Command.

The reason for developing this computer Language was to create a simple computer Language which was capable of performing all computer Language tasks. By keeping the number of Commands to a minimum and by keeping the syntax (Command structure) consistent across the Commands, Programmers could focus on solving problems rather than focusing on getting the Programming Language correct.

HI5IVE

Naming the Language

What would I name this new computer Language? Naming a computer Language is similar to naming a baby – too many options and most of them not quite what you had in mind.

Let's look at the names of some computer Languages, including the most popular ones.

COBOL is an acronym meaning COmmon Business Oriented Language (or COmmon Businessman's Oriented Language in UK). Ada was named for Ada Lovelace. She was the first Programmer.

C# (pronounced C-Sharp) is an enhanced version of C++ which is an enhanced version of C. C was so named because it was developed from a Language called B which was a stripped down version of a Language called BCPL which is an acronym for Basic Combined Programming Language. So, C# is an acronym of an acronym.

Javascript is a version of ECMAScript. ECMA is an acronym for European Computer Manufacturers Association which is responsible for the syntax of ECMAScript. Javascript was originally called Mocha, then LiveScript, then Javascript. The Java part of Javascript may have been taken from the Java Programming Language (though those two Languages have little, if anything, in common). The script part of the Language tells us it's a scripting Language – a Language commonly used to do simple tasks. Java was originally called Oak (after a tree), then Green, then Java (just a catchy name).

Python was named after Monty Python's Flying Circus. PHP was originally an acronym for Personal Home Page. Now it is an acronym for PHP: Hypertext Preprocessor. Perl was originally named Pearl, after the

HI5IVE

gem, but there was already a Programming Language named Pearl, so the name was shortened to Perl. Ruby was similarly named after another gem.

BASIC is an acronym which stands for Beginner's All-Purpose Symbolic Instruction Code. SQL stands for Structured Query Language.

So, many computer Language names are acronyms which often (but not always) describe the Language, though sometimes in terms only a Programmer can love. Sometimes the acronyms are catchy, sometimes not so much. Other computer Language names describe the Language without being acronyms. Yet others are just catchy words or phrases. And a handful are named after people, pets, or trees.

I originally called this computer Language 5IVECL. 5IVE for the number of Commands and CL being an acronym for Command Language. I later shortened this to 5IVE. I also considered naming this Language KISL as an acronym for Keep It Simple Language.

Acronyms are never simple as most acronyms stand for multiple combinations of words. I was tempted to call it Simplest, just to describe it. However, there's a computer Language called SiMPLE which is an acronym for Simple Modular Programming Language & Environments, and Simplest and SiMPLE are just too close. Unlike baby names, names for computer Programming Languages need to be unique.

My grandpa had a saying, "It's just like down home". "Just like down home" can mean, "It's just like I remember when I was a kid." My grandpa used "It's just like down home" to mean "It's ideal". So, I considered calling this Programming Language DownHome, since, at least in my mind, it's ideal. I could have made it an acronym and call it JLDH, but acronyms are never simple and JLDH is not catchy.

After many labor pains with this Language, at least with deciding what to name it, I've decided to name it **HI5IVE**. It now has more than 5 Commands, so I've added HI to express that it's a higher version or a hybrid of the original version. The original intent was to reduce a computer Language to the least number of Commands. That was accomplished, but one Command did no work and one other did the bulk of the work. To even things out and make the Language more useable and easier to remember, more Commands were added. **HI5IVE** is also a positive phrase meaning, everything's alright. **HI5IVE** is catchy and easy to remember, even if nobody remembers what it stands for.

HI5IVE

Sometimes people change their names as they grow older, sometimes when they get married, sometimes when they become famous. Perhaps **HI5IVE**'s name will also change with time.

At this point, **HI5IVE** is a Pseudo or Meta Language. It has not been implemented as an actual computer Programming Language yet – 2015. However, it is still very useful for communicating computer code with non-Programmers. It is also very useful for describing business Language in terms that Programmers can easily understand. It also helps Programmers remember the basics of what computer Programming Languages do which comes in handy when other Programming Languages (or Programs written in them) become complex and confusing. And it can help Programmers restructure complex code; making the code simpler, more understandable, and easier to maintain.

Making it Simpler
Reducing the Number of Commands

Some Languages call their action Statements Commands.[1] Others call them Statements. Wikipedia in the previous footnote calls them Instructions. I prefer Commands since that tells you they do something. I originally called them Decrees. In COBOL the Command Statement is called a Sentence and a sentence starts with a Command.

Depending on the version and the way you count them, COBOL has about 60 Commands, all with different sentence formats. C# has about 20 Commands which it calls Statements. Javascript also has about 20 Statements. Java might be said to only have a dozen Statements. Then there are Languages like FORTH (now obsolete) where you can define new Routines, each of which can become a new Command.

All these Commands or Statements can be reduced to the following 5 Commands: Comment, Move, Perform, If, and Define. I'll include a quick overview of these Commands here and describe each in more detail later.

Comment

There is not a Command for Comment in most computer Languages. REM is used in BASIC; =begin ... =end is used in Ruby. However, good Programming technique includes a reasonable number of somewhat clear

---

[1] Comparison of Programming Languages – Basic Instructions:
https://en.wikipedia.org/wiki/Comparison_of_programming_Languages_(basic_instructions)

HI5IVE

summary Comments spread throughout the Program at points where the Comments are helpful.

Comments aren't really a Command, they're just Notes. Many computer Languages have their own unique way of denoting a Comment. Using /* to start the Comment and */ to end the Comment is the most common method for doing this.[2] To make the syntax of **HI5IVE** consistent, even with Comments, I created the Comment Command.

HI5IVE uses **Comment** to denote Comments. **EndComment** ends the Comment.

Move

Read, Write, Move, Assign, Compute, =, Echo, Display, and Print are all Commands which move data from one place to another. Usually the data is kept in both the original location/variable and in the new location/variable, but not always.

HI5IVE uses **Move** for all these Statements. **Move** can be thought of as an ETL Statement. ETL stands for Extract, Transform, and Load. **Move** extracts data from one place, optionally transforms it, and loads it into another place. **EndMove** ends the **Move** Command.

Perform

Perform, Run, Exec, Execute, Go, Try, Call, Loop, For, and While are all Commands which perform Routines (a Routine may be an entire Program) or Commands. Usually the Routine returns to the next Command after Perform, but not always. The Routine may be performed zero[3], one, or many times. These Commands are also known as looping Commands.

HI5IVE uses **Perform** for all these Statements. **EndPerform** ends the **Perform** Command. In **HI5IVE**, the Routine always returns to the Command after **EndPerform**.

---

[2] Comments in various Languages:
https://en.wikipedia.org/wiki/Comparison_of_programming_languages_(syntax)#Comments

[3] Routine performed zero times: Yes, zero means the routine isn't performed, but that is usually due to conditions which can vary. So, in a different pass through these commands, the Routine may be performed.

HI5IVE

If

If, Switch, Case, and Branch are all Commands which make a decision as to what to do. Loop, For, and While also contain decision logic, as does Perform.

HI5IVE uses **If** for all these Statements. **EndIf** ends the **If** Statement. **Else** may be contained within the **If** Statement. Looping Commands need to be written as two Commands in **HI5IVE** – **If** and **Perform** – if they contain decision logic.

Define

Some Languages use Statements like Def to define variables. Some also use the type of the variable to define a variable – e.g. Int, Str, Array. Some Languages have a separate section where variables are defined. While others don't bother to define variables or leave the definition as optional.

Other things besides variables are defined in Programming Languages – Routines, Data Structures including Files, etc.

HI5IVE used **Define** to define everything that needs to be defined. **EndDefine** ends the **Define** Statement.

The types of things which can be defined, can be summarized as Variables, Data (Files, Tables, Rows, Columns), Routines (including Programs), Commands, Presentation Layers (including pictures, graphics, website display Languages including HTML and CSS, reports, forms), Sounds, Security, and People.

We also need to be able to define groups. These could be groups of variables, such as arrays or structures. These could be groups of data. These could be groups of some combination of Security and People.

To make Variables more generic, to cover more situations, I'll call them Elements.

To keep things straight I'll refer to Files and Tables as Files. Elements will include variables, constants, columns in tables, and fields in files. Files also include I/O devices – Printer, Screen, Keyboard, Mouse, USB port, etc. Files also include websites. We also need to be able to define locations such as file paths, positions in files, and positions in arrays. These will all be referred to as locations.

I'll also combine Presentation Layers and Sounds into Media (since some media contain both).

Routines and Commands could be combined, but I'll keep them separate.

So, the final list is Elements, Files, Routines, Commands, Media, Security, People, and Groups. There may be others, but this list covers most things.

Since **Define** does the bulk of the work defining a variety of things, I replaced **Define** with separate Commands for each generic thing which can be defined – **Command**, **Element**, **File**, **Group**, **Location**, **Media**, **Person**, **Routine**, and **Security**. **Element**, **File**, **Location**, and **Media** were still similar enough that I combined those back into the **Define** Command.

That resulted in the final list of 10 Commands for defining things: **Command**, **Comment**, **Define**, **Group**, **If**, **Move**, **Perform**, **Person**, **Routine**, and **Security**.

HI5IVE

The Command Format

Originally, each Command Statement in **HI5IVE** consisted of the same seven parts, some of which were optional. Today, that basic Command format still holds, but there's more flexibility to it. The basic format is now:

- Each Command starts with the Command and ends with EndCommand. So, **Comment** starts with **Comment** and ends with **EndComment**.
- The basic structure of a Command Statement is best illustrated by the **Move** and **Define** Commands. **Move** source *To* result *Through* transformation **EndMove**. **Define** name **As** type *Options* options **EndDefine**. The Command is followed the origin of the information or the name of something being defined. This is followed by a keyword or preposition to make the Command more readable. That keyword is followed by the result or type of object being defined. That is followed by another keyword to make the Command readable. That keyword is followed by the options or other information for the Command. The last keyword and the options which follow it are usually optional. The Command is ended with EndCommand.
- The bolding of the Command and the EndCommand are only for clarity. The bolding would be done automatically by the Programming Language editor. The italicizing is also for clarity and would also be done automatically by the editor.
- HI5IVE keeps the Command structure consistent, without making it rigid. For instance, HI5IVE is not case sensitive. You can say **Define, define, DEFINE,** or **DeFINE.** You can also say **EndDefine, End-Define, End_Define,** or **End Define.**

HI5IVE

The format of each Command follows. In the following chapters, the Commands are described in more detail.

Command new command *Is* new statement *Does* Routine **EndCommand**

Comment Comment **EndComment**

Define object *As* object type *Options* options **EndDefine**

If condition *Then* commands *Else* commands **EndIf**

Group group *Parts* parts *Relationships* relationships **EndGroup**

Move equation *To* result *Through* transformation **EndMove**

Perform performer *Using* parameters *Looping* conditions **EndPerform**

Person who *Is* description *Attributes* attributes **EndPerson**

Routine routine *Using* parameters *Commands* commands **EndRoutine**

Security role *For* person *Access* object accesstype level **EndSecurity**

Command

Command new command *Is* new statement *Does* routine
EndCommand

New Commands should only be created after much contemplation as to how useful the Command will be, whether this is only a one-time need, and investigation into if and how this functionality might already exist in **HI5IVE**.

New Command is the name of the new Command. New Statement is the structure of the new Statement. Routine is the name of the Routine which you've created to carry out the Command.

Example:
Command Shape *Is* **Shape** shape *As* shape type *Options* options **EndShape** *Does* ShapeRoutine **EndCommand**
Note: In this example, **Group** might be used instead of creating a new Command called **Shape**. **Group** would be used by grouping locations together. Locations would be defined with **Define**.

Comment

Comment comment **EndComment**

Add Comments where appropriate. Comments may apply to a Routine, to a set of Commands, to an element or file or something else. It can be helpful to state what the Comment applies to within the Comment.

Example:
Comment The Draw Box Routine draws a box **EndComment**

Define

Define object *As* object type *Options* options **EndDefine**

The types of objects which can be defined are Elements (Variables, Constants, Columns, Fields, etc.), Files (Files, Tables, Devices, Websites, etc.), Locations (Positions, Bookmarks, File Paths, etc.), Media (Pictures, Graphics, Website Display Languages including HTML and CSS, Reports, Forms, Sounds, etc.), and Routines. Options includes more information about the object, such as data type and length for Elements.

Examples:
Define Element A *As* Element *Options* Datatype=Numeric, Length=9, Decimal Places=2 **EndDefine**
Define File B *As* File *Options* Filetype=Table, Access=Input, Location=Location C **EndDefine**
Define Location C *As* Location *Options* Location Type=File Path **EndDefine**
Define Media D *As* Media *Options* Media Type=Sound **EndDefine**

If

If condition *Then* commands *Else* commands **EndIf**

The **If** Command allows a Routine to perform Commands either optionally or conditionally. Condition specifies the condition when these Commands are performed. The condition is usually something like A=B but can be more complicated like A=B and C not = D. Parentheses are used to group conditions as in A=B and (C not = D or C=E) to eliminate ambiguity as to which condition is tested in combination with which other conditions(s). When the condition is met, the Then Commands are performed. When the condition is not met, the Else Commands are performed.

The Else keyword and following Commands are optional. When Else is specified, Then and following Commands are optional.

Example:
If A=B *Then* **Move** C *To* D **EndMove** *Else* **Move** C *To* E **EndMove** **EndIf**

If Commands are usually formatted over several lines using indentation to make them more readable:

If A=B
Then
    Move C To D **EndMove**
Else
    Move C to E **EndMove**
EndIf

Group

Group group *Parts* parts *Relationships* relationships **EndGroup**

Group combines objects. Groups include Arrays, Data Structures, Shapes, and Themes.

Examples:
Group Array A *Parts* A *Relationships* Index=Index I, Occurs=100 **EndGroup**
Group Structure C *Parts* A, B *Relationships* A.Index=Index I, A.Occurs=100 **EndGroup**

Parts of groups can be referred to as Group.Part. Using the examples above, we could refer to Array A.A, Structure C.A(1), and Structure C.B.

Move

Move equation *To* result *Through* transformation **EndMove**

Move extracts data from one place, optionally transforms it, and loads it into another place. Transformation may be a Routine, mask, style, filter, etc. Filtering is usually accomplished by placing **Move** within **If** or **Perform**, but **If** and **Perform** can be placed within **Move** to act as filters just as easily.

Examples:
Move A *To* B *Through* Square Root **EndMove**
Move A *To* B *Through* From Mask=yyyymmdd To Mask=dd/mmm/yyyy **EndMove**
Move A *To* B *Through* Filter=Sort **EndMove**
Move File A *To* Printer **EndMove**

Perform

Perform performer *Using* parameters *Looping* conditions **EndPerform**

Perform performs a Routine or Commands. Routines sometimes need to be passed parameters (usually objects – Variables, Files, etc.). Routines or Commands can be performed 0, 1, or many times, depending on the conditions stated after *Looping*. **Perform** can be placed within **If**, rather than using *Looping*.

Both *Using* parameters and *Looping* conditions are optional.

Examples:
Perform Print Routine **EndPerform**
Perform Print Routine *Using* File A **EndPerform**
Perform Print Routine *Using* File A *Looping* from 1 to 9 **EndPerform**
Perform Print Routine *Using* File A *Looping* until Condition=Out of Paper **EndPerform**
Perform
    Move A *To* B **EndMove**
    Move C *To* D **EndMove**
EndPerform

Person

Person who *Is* description *Attributes* attributes **EndPerson**

Person describes a person. A person may be a computer user, a contact, somebody else, a pet, or other entity. Description is a text description. Attributes are descriptive attributes.

Example:
Person Dale Stubbart *Is* The author of HI5IVE *Attributes* Hair Color=Brown, Eye Color=Hazel **EndPerson**

Routine

Routine routine *Using* parameters *Commands* commands **EndRoutine**

Routine is used to define a Routine. Parameters can be passed to Routines.

Example:
Routine Routine A *Using* A, B *Commands*
Comment Routine A replaces B with A and replaces A with 5
EndComment
Move A To B **EndMove**
Move 5 to A **EndMove**
EndRoutine

Security

Security role *For* subject *Access* object accesstype level **EndSecurity**

Security assigns security for an object to a subject. The subject can be anything which is defined – a Person, File, Group, Routine, etc. Accesstype includes Read, Write, Create, Delete, and Update. Level sets different clearance levels. Level is optional.

Example:
Security Read Only Role *For* Dale Stubbart *Access* Object=File A, Access Type=Read, Level=Top **EndSecurity**

HI5IVE

Summary

At this point, **HI5IVE** is a Pseudo or Meta Language. The best use for **HI5IVE** is to keep decision logic clear. **If**, when used properly can clarify to Users and Programmers exactly what the decision logic is. **HI5IVE** is also useful for writing Program specs and for communicating to a non-Programmer what a Program is doing.

HI5IVE is simple, yet flexible. The number of Commands can be kept to a minimum, or can be expanded as needed for clarification. The basic format of each Command is simple. At the same time, each Command is powerful.

Including EndCommand, tells everybody exactly where each Command ends. For simple logic, this could be omitted. But for more complex logic it is necessary. EndCommand has been retained for clarity for all Commands, everywhere in HI5IVE, even when the logic is simple. This helps people avoid the tendency to omit it in complex logic, making the complex logic unclear.

HI5IVE could be developed into a functioning Programming Language, if one knew how to do that and was so inclined. The first step would be to develop the **Define** Command, then **Routine**, then **Command**.

Simple Tutorials to Programming Languages, often include an example of an "Hello World" Program or Routine. Why "Hello World", I'm not sure. But usually, it's a simple Routine, displaying some of the Commands of the Programming Language. It's a way of showing the reader how the Commands might work together.

HI5IVE

You could probably care less about displaying or printing Hello World. Instead, this example Program will show you how to change the theme in the files you have selected.

Routine Change Theme *Using* Files.Selected *Commands*
    Group New Theme *Parts* Background Color, Font, Border *Relationships* Background Color=Blue, Font=TimesNewRoman Bold 12px, Border=Solid **EndGroup**
    Group Old Theme *Parts* Background Color, Font, Border *Relationships* Background Color=Pink, Font=New Theme.Font, Border=Dashed **EndGroup**
    Move New Theme to Old Theme through Files.Selected **EndMove**
EndRoutine

If you wanted to do something more complicated, you might think about using **Perform** … **EndPerform** to enclose several **Move** (and possibly other) Commands.

Since the above example didn't show the **If** or **Perform** Commands, here is a Hello World Routine that does that. This doesn't show all the Commands. I'll leave that to your imagination.

Routine Hello World *Using* User *Commands*
    Person Joe **EndPerson**
    Person Jane **EndPerson**
    Group Joe Theme *Parts* Background Color, Font, Border *Relationships* Background Color=Blue, Font=Times New Roman Bold 12px, Border=Solid **EndGroup**
    Group Jane Theme *Parts* Background Color, Font, Border *Relationships* Background Color=Pink, Font=Joe Theme.Font, Border=Dashed **EndGroup**
    If User=Joe
    Then
      Perform
        Move "Hello World" to Default Output Device *Through* Theme=Joe Theme **EndMove**
        Looping from 1 to 3
      EndPerform
    Else

HI5IVE

    Perform

        Move "Hello World" to Default Output Device *Through* Theme=Jane Theme **EndMove**

        Looping until Condition=Escape Key Pressed

      EndPerform

    EndIf

  EndRoutine

HI5IVE

About the Author

Dale Stubbart lives and writes in the Pacific Northwest (USA). He writes Fantasy, Spiritual, and Computer Books. He also writes Love Stories.

This Computer Book explains the elements which make up Programming Languages. His understanding of the basic commonality underlying all computer languages helps him become an expert in any language quickly. His hope is the HI5IVE will help everyone understand computer languages better and that communication between end-users and programmers will be facilitated through HI5IVE. HI5IVE has been designed. His hope is that it will one day be implemented as an actual computer language.

Perhaps it will be incorporated into his idea for a Right-Brained Computer. That book will be available at Amazon sometime in 2016.

You can find more of his stories at Amazon, at YellowBearJourneys.com, and at PrincessTigerLily.com/sss.

Dale Stubbart
March 2013

About the Author